The American Pentecostal Movement

A Bibliographical Essay

by

David W. Faupel

Occasional Bibliographic Papers of the B.L. Fisher

Library #2

First Fruits Press
Wilmore, Kentucky
c2012

asburyseminary.edu
800.2ASBURY
204 North Lexington Avenue
Wilmore, Kentucky 40390

First Fruits
THE ACADEMIC OPEN PRESS OF ASBURY SEMINARY

ISBN: 9780984738663

The American Pentecostal Movement: a Bibliographical Essay, by David W. Faupel.
First Fruits Press, © 2012
B. L. Fisher Library, Asbury Theological Seminary, © 1972

Digital version at http://place.asburyseminary.edu/firstfruitspapers/4/

For all other uses, contact:

First Fruits Press
B.L. Fisher Library
Asbury Theological Seminary
204 N. Lexington Ave.
Wilmore, KY 40390
http://place.asburyseminary.edu/firstfruits

Faupel, David W.
    The American Pentecostal movement : a bibliographical essay / by David W. Faupel..
    Wilmore, Ky. : First Fruits Press, c2012.
    Reprint. Previously published: Wilmore, Ky. : B. L. Fisher Library, Asbury Theological Seminary, c1972.
    60 p. ; 21 cm. -- (Occasional bibliographic papers of the B. L. Fisher Library ; no. 2)
    ISBN: 9780984738724 (pbk.)
    1. Pentecostal churches—Bibliography. 2. Pentecostal churches—Periodicals—Bibliography. I. Title. II. B. L. Fisher Library. Occasional papers ; no. 2.
    BX8762 .F38 2012

Cover design by Haley Hill

asburyseminary.edu
800.2ASBURY
204 North Lexington Avenue
Wilmore, Kentucky 40390

First Fruits
THE ACADEMIC OPEN PRESS OF ASBURY SEMINARY

THE AMERICAN PENTECOSTAL MOVEMENT

A Bibliographical Essay

THE AMERICAN PENTECOSTAL MOVEMENT

A BIBLIOGRAPHICAL ESSAY

by

David W. Faupel

The Second in a Series of
"Occasional Bibliographic Papers
of the B. L. Fisher Library"

B. L. Fisher Library
Asbury Theological Seminary
Wilmore, Kentucky 40390
1972

This Essay is a Revised Version
of the Text Published Originally in
the 1972 PROCEEDINGS of the
American Theological Library Association

Price

1 - 10 copies $2.00 each
11 or more copies $1.50 each

plus postage and handling
unless payment accompanies order.

Copies may be ordered from:

David W. Faupel
B. L. Fisher Library
Asbury Theological Seminary
Wilmore, Kentucky   40390

PREFACE

This project was deemed appropriate to follow Donald Dayton's The American Holiness Movement: A Bibliographic Introduction, which was the first publication in the B. L. Fisher Library bibliographic series. A summary of this essay on Pentecostalism was presented to the twenty-sixth annual conference of the American Theological Library Association held at Waterloo, Ontario, in June 1972. This is a revised text of the essay as it appears in the 1972 Proceedings of the Association.

When leaders of the Society for Pentecostal Studies learned of the proposed project, they expressed interest in this effort to gain bibliographic control of the extensive literature in the Pentecostal Movement. As a result this paper is published as the Second Occasional Paper in the B. L. Fisher Library Bibliographic Series and as the first publication of the Society for Pentecostal Studies.

I wish to express appreciation to Peter VandenBerge, then vice-president of ATLA, for providing a place on the program for the paper and to the Association for granting permission to print the paper as a monograph.

I am indebted to several colleagues on the faculty of Asbury Theological Seminary: Delbert R. Rose, Professor of Biblical Theology and Historian for the Christain Holiness Association; Kenneth C. Kinghorn, Professor of Church History; Robert A. Traina, Academic Dean; Miss Susan A. Schultz, Director of Library Services; and Donald W. Dayton, former Acquisitions Librarian, for their encouragement and critical evaluation of the manuscript.

I am also grateful to Vinson Synan, secretary of SPS and William Menzies, former president of SPS for their guidance and encouragement in the initial stages of the project. In addition, they, along with Zenas Bicket, Donald Bowdle, Steven Durasoff, William MacDonald, and Russell Spittler, all members of SPS, read the manuscript, providing many helpful suggestions and corrections. Oral Roberts University graciously made its Pentecostal Collection available to me, and Mrs. Juanita Raudszus, ORU's Learning Resources Librarian, provided several bibliographic tools which saved many hours of labor.

Finally, I wish to express my thanks to several members of the B. L. Fisher Library staff: Len Chester typed the first draft from a difficult manuscript; Mrs. Esther Richter prepared the final copy for printing; and David Bundy and Mrs. Esther James did much of the editing and proofreading.

The literature mentioned in this paper is scattered throughout the United States; therefore, checking all data for bibliographical accuracy proved to be a problem. I accept full responsibility for any errors which may appear, and would greatly appreciate receiving information on any inaccuracy discovered by the readers.

David W. Faupel
Public Services Librarian
    and Instructor in Biblio-
    graphy and Research
B. L. Fisher Library
Asbury Theological Seminary

CONTENTS

INTRODUCTION

In presenting a bibliographical introduction to the Pentecostal Movement several decisions had to be made.

First there is the problem of definition. William Menzies, in his work Anointed to Serve: the Story of the Assemblies of God (Springfield, Mo.: Gospel Publishing House, 1971) writes:

> The Pentecostal Movement is that group of sects within the Christian Church which is characterized by the belief that the occurrence mentioned in Acts 2 on the Day of Pentecost not only signaled the birth of the church, but described an experience available to believers in all ages. The experience of an enduement with power, called the "baptism in the Holy Spirit" is believed to be evidenced by the accompanying sign of "speaking with other tongues as the Spirit gives utterance" (p. 9)

Menzies suggests such a definition is inadequate to measure the complete spread of the Pentecostal Movement. Two recent developments must be noted. First the "Pentecostal experience" has spread to the historic churches, both Catholic and Protestant. To date no one has been able to measure accurately its growth and influence. However, this phase of the Pentecostal Movement has produced a great deal of literature which must be noted to make this essay complete. A second development is the "Jesus Movement." Those associated with this movement stand largely outside of organized Christianity though many hold to the Pentecostal doctrinal distinctive. These two trends are noted in this essay. but emphasis is placed on the literature of those groups which fall within the bounds of the definition cited.

The Pentecostal Movement became international almost immediately. This essay makes little attempt to trace the literature outside the United States, except in those cases that have a direct bearing on the American scene.

A final point of discussion before beginning the writing of the essay is stating criteria for organization of the literature.

The majority of scholarly works on the Pentecostal Movement are written from an historical perspective. I have been influenced by these works in my general approach to the literature--grouping the material around major trends and controversies as they appear historically within the Movement. I feel that such an approach does the most justice to the literature, enables the reader to gain a better understanding of the Movement, and points out quickly the gaps that need further research.

WORLD-WIDE SURVEYS

The starting point for understanding the Pentecostal Movement is John Thomas Nichol, Pentecostalism (New York: Harper and Row, 1966)   It has been reissued in paperback by the Logos Press of Plainfield, New Jersey. with a new title, The Pentecostals. This work, originally a Ph.D. dissertation at Boston University, gives a bird's-eye view of the growth of Pentecostalism on the world scene.

Nichol's major contribution to existing literature is that he has shown the rise of the Pentecostal Movement internationally in relation to its American origins.

The chief weakness of the book is his treatment of individual denominations in the Pentecostal Movement. He groups them by size rather than by their organizational structure or doctrinal emphasis. His approach shows little understanding for the factors leading to the existence of so many Pentecostal denominations.[1]

---

1. E. L. Moore in an M.A. thesis, "A Handbook of Pentecostal Denominations in the United States, lists over forty separate Pentecostal bodies. Walter J. Hollenweger, in his newly published work, The Pentecostals: The Charismatic Movement in the Churches, p. 29, claims to know of the existence of at least two hundred Pentecostal bodies in the United States. (Many are no larger than a handful of churches.)

Though Nichol provides little new material, he has
brought together the best of previous Pentecostal
scholarship, and, for this reason, his book serves
as an excellent introduction to the Movement. His
nine-page classified bibliography is helpful for
further studies.

Without doubt the most comprehensive work on Pentecostalism has been done by Walter J. Hollenweger,
formerly Executive Secretary of the Department of
Studies in Evangelism of the World Council of
Churches. He is currently professor of mission at
the University of Birmingham in England. Like Nichol, he is the son of a Pentecostal minister; he
pastored a Pentecostal church himself for ten years.

His multi-volume Zurich dissertation,"Handbuch der
Pfingstbewegung," ['65]available on microfilm from
ATLA Board of.Microtext, is a goldmine of historical, doctrinal, and statistical information on Pentecostal groups throughout the world.

Hollenweger's work is difficult to assess. The size
and scope of his work is staggering. However, one
gains the distinct impression that his analysis
rests as much on his presuppositions as on the data
he has collected. The work must be a starting point
for all future research.

Hollenweger has summarized his work in Enthusias-
tisches Christentum: die Pfingstbewegung in Ge-
schichte und Gegenwart (Zurich: Rolf Brockhaus
Wuppental, 1966)   This was recently translated into
English as The Pentecostals: the Charismatic Movement in the Church (Minneapolis: Augsburg, 1972)
Especially helpful are his notes at the end of each
chapter and a thirty-five page annotated bibliography.

A third work on International Pentecostalism is
Nils Bloch-Hoell, The Pentecostal Movement; its
Origin, Development and Distinctive Character (Oslo:
Universitetsforlaget; London: Allen and Unwin; and
New York: Humanities Press, 1964). This work, a
revised English translation of a 1956 Norwegian
work Pinsebevegelsen, is currently the most comprehensive work on Pentecostalism in Europe that has
been published in English. The author's analysis,
especially of American Pentecostal doctrine and
distinctives, reflects his European background.

Major concern has been expressed by some American

Pentecostal scholars concerning Bloch-Hoell's understanding of the origin and development of Pentecostalism in the U. S. However, Walter Hollenweger
has stated that his description of the Azusa Street
Revival is the most extensive and accurate to date.[2]

Bloch-Hoell concludes his work with fifty-five pages
of bibliographical notes that are most helpful in
giving additional detail that is not normally located elsewhere. His bibliography contains mainly
non-English items which are not listed in most bibliographies on Pentecostalism.

CLASSIFICATION OF AMERICAN PENTECOSTAL GROUPS

Everett L. Moore, "Handbook of Pentecostal Denominations in the United States" (Pasadena: Pasadena
College, June 1954), an unpublished M.A. thesis,
must be first considered.[3]

Moore's work claims no profundity. but does render a
practical service by listing forty Pentecostal denominations, organized around the following cate-
gories:

1. Those denominations which hold a Keswick
    view of sanctification.
2. Those denominations which hold a Holiness
    view of "entire sanctification."
3. Those denominations which hold a "Jesus
    Only" view of the God-head.

---

2. Walter S. Hollenweger "A Black Pentecostal Con-
    cept; A Forgotten Chapter in Black History,"
Concept, Special Issue 30, June 1970, Papers from
the Department on Studies in Evangelism, World Council of Churches, p. 14.

3. Because Moore's "Handbook" makes this analysis,
    in addition to its obvious use as a reference
tool, serious consideration should be given to up-
date this work and make it available in published
form. It also serves to remind us that the time
has come for the Pentecostal bodies, as listed in
Frank S. Mead, Handbook of Denominations in the
United States (Nashville: Abingdon Press, 1970, 5th
ed.) and the Yearbook of American Churches, to be
reorganized along the lines suggested by Moore.

He concludes with a brief appendix on the Latter
Rain Movement.

For each denomination he gives a brief historical
sketch, its doctrinal statement and ecclesiastical
structure.

Moore quite rightly suggests that:

> For the first fourteen years, the Movement
> had no standard of doctrine because its mem-
> bership was drawn from various backgrounds,
> held together only by faith in speaking in
> other tongues. It was during these years
> that various groups found small nuclei from
> which later grew the numerous Pentecostal
> Churches today in existence (p. 20)

In an analysis of Moore's work, one quickly dis-
covers the several factors which led to the rise
of so many Pentecostal groups.

First were the doctrinal divisions mentioned above.
But within these theological groupings, several
other factors emerged to cause further splittings:
(1) Race: This is such an important factor that I
have elected to do a separate division of my essay
on this issue, in addition to the theological
groupings. (2) Church Government: Within each
theological grouping, congregational, presbyterian,
and episcopal forms of church polity emerged. (3)
Strong personalities: A. J. Tomlinson and Aimee
Semple McPherson are prominent examples of personalities who caused further divisions.

Klaude Kendrick, The Promise Fulfilled: A History
of the Modern Pentecostal Movement (Springfield,
Mo.: Gospel Publishing House, 1961) is also important for a study of American Pentecostalism. Kendrick is the first to group Pentecostal bodies by
the issues that were determinative in forming separate denominations.

Wesleyan Perfectionist Groups

With the appearance of Vinson Synan, The Holiness-
Pentecostal Movement in the United States (Grand
Rapids: Eerdmans, 1971) Pentecostal scholarship
has moved into a new phase of development. It
is the first analysis of the Movement seen from
the perspective of a major theological tradition

within the Movement.[4]

Synan spends a great deal of space tracing the origins of the Pentecostal Movement back through the American Holiness Movement, Methodism, Anglicanism, and finally to the Roman Church. Contending that Pentecostalism arose outside the influence of Reformed theology, Synan marshalls his evidence to support the thesis that the Pentecostal Movement in its original form represents a division within the Holiness Movement. Thus, in his view, those Pentecostal denominations which hold to a "finished work" view of sanctification are seen as the first major split in Pentecostal theology.[5]

---

4. Two other works are scheduled to be written on major segments within Pentecostalism: David Reed, "Historical and Theological Origins of the 'Oneness' or 'Jesus Only' Movement"(Boston: Boston University Ph.D. thesis topic) and Garnet Pike, "Historical Study of Black Pentecostals" (Vanderbilt, Ph.D. thesis topic)

5. The most extensive discussion of the issues involved regarding the doctrine of entire sanctification in its Pentecostal historical context is Irvine John Harrison's unpublished Th.D. dissertation, "A History of the Assemblies of God" (Berkeley: Baptist Divinity School, 1954), p. 126 ff.

He notes that William H. Durham, a Baptist Englishman came to the Azusa Street Revival to teach his doctrine of the "finished work of Christ." Harrison quotes J Roswell Flower, an early leader of the Assemblies of God:

Durham carried his message to Los Angeles and preached it in Azusa Street...When he was turned out of Azusa Street, he continued his ministry by word of mouth and printed page in other quarters until his death. The emphasis he gave to the finished work of Christ was accented by ridicule of the Holiness teaching on sanctification as the necessary work of grace, and a prerequisite to the Baptism of the Holy Ghost. This divorced him from the sympathies of the Holiness groups. .on the other hand, those of Baptistic backgrounds readily accepted his teaching. The contro-

Synan's strongest argument for his case is his demonstration that early leaders in the Movement were from the Holiness Movement and continued to hold that position after they embraced the new Pentecostal doctrine.

---

versy over this point of doctrine became so acute that the Holiness groups in the Southeast, for the most part, withdrew into themselves and discouraged fellowship with the Movement in other parts of the country (p. 132)

Two additional unpublished theses provide further background material concerning the origins of Pentecostalism: Calvin Carmen, "The Posture of Pentecostalism in View of the Crucial Issues of the Fundamentalist--Neo-Evangelical Debate" (Springfield, Mo.: Central Bible Institute, M.A. thesis, 1965), and Frank C. Masserano, "A Study of Worship Forms in the Assemblies of God" (Princeton, N. J.: Princeton Theological Seminary, M.Th. thesis, 1966)

Masserano contends that while the Holiness Movement played a large part in the rise of Pentecostalism, the Movement must be viewed as having broader origins. He writes:

While the Pentecostal Holiness Church established a doctrine of three blessings (i.e., salvation, sanctification, and the Holy Spirit Baptism), for most Pentecostals, the sanctification terminology and concepts were transferred to a Keswick interpretation of the Holy Spirit Baptism.. (p. 44) the Keswick doctrine of the baptism of the Holy Spirit as taught by D. L. Moody, R. A. Torrey and A. B. Simpson was to be combined with the Holiness emphasis on sanctification and enthusiasm in defining of Pentecostal doctrine (p. 45)

In addition to these factors, Pentecostalism was rejected outright by most Holiness groups. Also Holiness-Pentecostal groups have been largely confined to southeastern United States. (See Menzies, Anointed to Serve, pp. 80, 81.) Synan needs to be taken seriously. His thesis will, no doubt, be debated among Pentecostals for years to come.

Charles F. Parham,[6] the first 20th century person
to articulate the Pentecostal doctrine that
speaking in other tongues was the initial evidence
of the baptism in the Holy Spirit, was originally a
Methodist lay minister. Synan clearly demonstrates
that Parham embraced the doctrine and received the
experience of entire sanctification. Likewise, W.
J. Seymour, a student of Parham, and the leader of
the Azusa Street Revival taught the doctrine of
entire sanctification.[7]

The evidence tends to support Synan's thesis. Pentecostal theology was developed in the context of

---

6. For a biography of this man, see Sarah E. Par-
    ham, The Life of Charles F. Parham, Founder of
the Apostolic Faith Movement (Joplin, Mo.: Tri-
State Printing Co., 1930)   This apology by his
wife is obviously a highly biased account of his
life and ministry, but provides many interesting
details not found elsewhere.

7. The importance of the Azusa revival to the Pen-
    tecostal Movement cannot be over-emphasized.
Not only was it the spark that gave rise to the
Movement, but also almost all the issues which led
to the formation of the several separate denominational groups can be traced back to it. Those
issues were: (1) the dispute of the doctrine of
entire sanctification; (2) the Jesus Only, or Oneness doctrine; (3) the teaching of the Latter Rain
Covenant; and, (4) the formation of denominations
along racial lines.

For a firsthand report of the revival at Azusa
Street, one should consult Frank Bartleman, How
Pentecost Came to Los Angeles (Los Angeles: pri-
vately printed, 1928)   This account has been re-
printed in an abridged form under the title, What
Really Happened at "Azusa Street" by Voice Chris-
tian Publications in 1962. It is available at
Voice magazine, Box 672, North Ridge, California.

Also an interesting autobiography of the first person to speak in tongues under Parham's ministry is
Agnes N. O. LaBerge, What God Hath Wrought--Life
and Work of Mrs. Agnes N. O. LaBerge, nee Miss
Agnes N. Ozman (Chicago: Herald Publishing Co.
1921)

the Holiness Movement. He fails to account, however, for the other forces at work which quickly
attached themselves to the Pentecostal doctrines,
but rejected their holiness origins. Given this
historical situation at the time, it was probably
inevitable that the Movement divide over this issue.
The background of too many people coming into the
Pentecostal Movement at the time was too alien to
the teachings of the holiness traditions. Synan
also includes an excellent chapter on the black Pentecostals. I will refer to this in greater detail
later.

One of the largest and oldest holiness-pentecostal
churches is the Church of God (Cleveland, Tennessee)
The church traces its origins back to a conference
called at Barney Creek Meeting House in Monroe
County. Tennessee in 1886. There Richard G. Spur-
ling, a disenchanted Baptist, challenged the people
at the conference to organize "to take the New Testament as the only rule of faith and practice, and
to sit together as the Church of God to transact
business."[8]

Two denominational histories document the origin
and growth of this denomination. E. L. Simmons,
History of the Church of God (Cleveland, Tenn.:
Church of God Publishing House, 1938) is the first
of these. A second, more scholarly work appeared
in 1955, Charles W. Conn, Like a Mighty Army Moves
the Church of God (Cleveland, Tenn.: Church of God
Publishing House, 1955)

L. Howard Juillerat, Book of Minutes (Cleveland,
Tenn.: Church of God Publishing House, 1922) provides invaluable resource material on the beginnings
of this church.

Charles W. Conn, Pillars of Pentecost (Cleveland,
Tenn.: Pathway Press, 1959) provides additional historical data through biographical sketches of the
early leaders.

Additional early material may be gleaned from J. W.
Buckalew, Incidents in the Life of J. W. Buckalew
(Cleveland, Tenn.: Church of God Publishing House,
1920)

---

8. Kendrick, The Promise Fulfilled, p. 189.

A. J. Tomlinson, the man directly responsible for bringing the Church of God into the Pentecostal Movement, provides much interesting personal detail of the early life of the church in a diary. The diary has been edited by his son, Homer A. Tomlinson, Diary of A. J. Tomlinson, 3 Vols. (New York: Church of God World Headquarters, 1949-1955)

Tomlinson, a Bible salesman and itinerant preacher from Indiana, was asked to join the Church of God in 1903. He received the Pentecostal experience in 1908 at the Church of God's annual convention under the ministry of G. B. Cashwell, a leader of the Pentecostal Holiness Church.

For the next few years, Tomlinson enjoyed almost unlimited authority in the Church of God until he was impeached in 1923 for mishandling funds. He then left the church to form the Church of God of Prophecy. For his own reaction to factors bringing about the split, see his Answering the Call of God (Cleveland, Tenn.: White Wing Publishing House, n.d.).[9] Tomlinson claimed the churches which left with him comprised the original Church of God. Only for legal purposes was added the phrase "of Prophecy" to the name of his church.

Claiming the right to appoint his successor, Tomlinson designated his son, Homer, to succeed him as General Overseer, at his death in 1943.

Thirty-four of the forty-eight state overseers approved of this move. Threatened by another church split, Homer suggested that his younger brother Milton, a printer by trade, be put in charge. This move was approved by the dissenting overseers, and Milton was ordained Bishop. One of his first official acts as Bishop was to expel his brother Homer from the church.

Homer promptly founded the Church of God World Headquarters. Like his father before, he claimed that he represented the Church of God that was started in 1903 (i.e., the date his father joined the Church

---

9. E. L. Moore, "Handbook of Pentecostal Denominations," pp. 145-165, in describing the origins of various Pentecostal bodies, provides an excellent synopsis of what followed.

of God, Cleveland, Tenn.)   Homer's career has been dotted with the spectacular. He ran for President of the United States several times, and in the early sixties proclaimed himself king of the world. He tells his story in The Shout of a King (New York: The Church of God World Headquarters, 1965)

Another important denomination in this segment of the Pentecostal Movement is the Pentecostal Holiness Church.

Vinson Synan, author of The Holiness-Pentecostal Movement, is presently writing a history of the denomination. The standard history of the church to date has been Joseph E. Campbell, The Pentecostal Holiness Church 1898-1949, Its History and Background (Franklin Springs, Ga.: Publishing House of the Pentecostal Holiness Church, 1951) The work is based on a Th.D. thesis written at Union Seminary in Richmond, Virginia, in 1948.

Campbell devotes a good deal of space to the many social and theological forces which brought his church into existence. Much of this is a simple restatement of Niebuhr, Sweet, and others who have sought to explain the rise of sects on the American scene.

Campbell also places emphasis on the development of his denomination's structure. For the student interested in detailed historical background, the work will be helpful. However, little is done by way of analysis and evaluation of the significance of what has developed throughout its history. An important aspect of the book is an analytical bibliography of Pentecostal Holiness publications.

A number of biographies and autobiographies of early leaders provide added insight to the development of this church. These include: Joseph H. and Blanche L. King, Yet Speaketh; Memoirs of the Late Bishop Joseph H. King (Franklin Springs, Ga.: Publishing House of the Pentecostal Holiness Church, 1949); R. H. Lee and G. H. Montgomery, ed., Edward O. Reeves; His Life and Message (Franklin Springs, Ga.: Publishing House of the Pentecostal Holiness Church, 1940); A. E. Robinson, A Layman and the Book (Franklin Springs, Ga.: Publishing House of the Pentecostal Holiness Church, 1936); and Watson Sorrow, Some of My Experiences (Franklin Springs, Ga.: Publishing House of the Pentecostal Holiness Church, 1954) Watson Sorrow later founded The

Congregational Holiness Church. The most famous personage to emerge from the Pentecostal Holiness Church is Oral Roberts. His autobiography, The Call (New York: Doubleday and Co. 1972) relates why he left to return to the United Methodist Church.

A small denomination with historic roots back to the Azusa Street Revival is the Apostolic Faith Mission led by Florence L. Crawford. The denomination still functions in the northwest, with headquarters in Portland, Oregon. The history of the denomination is documented in A Historical Account of the Apostolic Faith, a Trinitarian Fundamental Evangelistic Organization (Portland, Ore.: Apostolic Faith Mission, 1965), and can be ordered from Apostolic Faith Publishing House, N. W. Sixth & Burnside, Portland, Oregon, 97209.

B. L. Cox, History and Doctrine of the Congregational Holiness Church (Greenwood, South Carolina: Congregational Holiness Church Publishing House, 1959) provides the basic study of this small denomination of some five thousand members which broke with the Pentecostal Holiness Church in 1920 over divine healing and church government. Cox's autobiography, My Life Story (Greenwood, South Carolina: Congregational Holiness Publishing House, 1959) gives additional information.

Luther Gibson, History of the Church of God Mountain Assembly (n.p. 1954), documents the history of the small Pentecostal denomination whose headquarters is in Jellico, Tenn. It dates back to 1906, but growth has been limited to Eastern Kentucky and Tennessee. This denomination is the only known Pentecostal group that allows its members the use of tobacco.

An extensive search failed to locate histories of the several smaller Holiness-Pentecostal denominations, for example, the Pentecostal Fire Baptized Holiness Church, Emmanuel Holiness Church, and the Fire Baptized Holiness Church of God of America.

Keswick Pentecostal Groups

To date no study has appeared that would parallel Synan's work and determine the influence of the Keswick faction on the Pentecostal Movement as a whole. The sources are so scattered that an attempt to mention them here would be beyond the limitations of this essay. The basic question to be answered in such a study is: Why did this segment of the Pentecostal Movement experience national growth from the beginning of the movement, while the gains of the Holiness tradition were contained largely to southeastern United States for almost fifty years?

Until such a study is made, one must wrestle with the contention made by Menzies that the Assemblies of God is "the most representative of the Pentecostal organizations, and can serve usefully as a microcosm of the Pentecostal Movement as a whole."[10]

The best sources for the early history of the Assemblies of God are J. Roswell Flower, "History of the Assemblies of God,' a set of unpublished class notes;[11] B. F Lawrence, The Apostolic Faith Restored (St. Louis: Gospel Publishing House, 1916); Stanley H. Frodsham, With Signs Following Rev ed. (Springfield, Mo.: Gospel Publishing House, 1946);[12] C. C. Burnett, In the Last Days; A History of the Assemblies of God (Springfield, Mo.: Gospel Publishing House, 1962); and, Carl Brumback, Suddenly From Heaven, a History of the Assemblies of God (Springfield, Mo.: Gospel Publishing House, 1961)

Flower, more than any other single person, has stamped his image on the direction taken by the Assemblies of God. His notes are largely an apology for the Assemblies of God, designed to give second generation Pentecostals an understanding of their

---

10. Menzies, Anointed to Serve, p. 10. He further points out in a footnote that others such as Bloch-Hoell, Nichol and Kelsey (all non-Assemblies of God men) have made the same claim for the Assemblies of God. By this, he means all of the issues and forces which have been brought to bear on any part of the Pentecostal Movement have at some point affected the Assemblies of God as well. Despite initial reservations, this writer has come to accept this as basically true.

11. Copies of this are kept at Central Bible College and Evangel College in Springfield, Mo.

12. This was published originally under the title, The Pentecostal Revival, in 1941.

origins and religious heritage. Though undocumented, these notes provide an excellent opportunity to study the reflections and analysis of an eyewitness. Flower was a pioneer in attempting to tie Pentecostalism to the main stream of church history. He notes that "tongues," the distinctive teaching of the Pentecostal Movement, have made periodic appearances throughout church history, the Pentecostal Movement being the first to identify this "gift" as evidence of the baptism in the Holy Spirit.[13]

Frodsham's work is also undocumented. As a long-time editor of the Pentecostal Evangel, he was in an excellent position to note significant trends in the denomination's growth. His work provides a helpful description of mission work overseas.

Brumback's work is the most scholarly of those mentioned. His greatest contributions are biographical sketches of many of the early leaders, preserving many of their significant statements.

Without question the historian par excellence in the Assemblies of God is William W. Menzies. His latest book, Anointed to Serve, the Story of the Assemblies of God (Springfield, Mo.: Gospel Publishing House, 1971) provides us with the most recent and comprehensive history of this denomination. The book is based on his Ph.D. dissertation, "The Assemblies of God, 1941-1967; The Consolidation of a Revival Movement" (University of Iowa, 1968)

As the dissertation title implies, Menzies focuses on the last thirty years of his denomination's history. Menzies argues that the denomination has undergone two major shifts since World War II.

First, the church moved from an era of isolation to a period of interdenominational cooperation. This is seen in their association with the National Association of Evangelicals, The World Pentecostal Fellowship, and the Pentecostal Fellowship of North America. Menzies contends that this movement is in

---

13. Bernard L. Bresson, Studies in Ecstasy (New York: Vantage Press, 1966) catalogues twenty-four movements and sects that have appeared between the second and the nineteenth centuries which practiced the gift of speaking in tongues.

line with the intent of early Pentecostal leaders.
At the beginning the leaders did not wish to form
a new denomination; rather, they desired to remain
in the historic denominations sharing their new
found experience with others. It ·as only as those
churches reacted against them that they were forced
to withdraw, form new denominations, and retreat to
isolation.

The second shift which Menzies notes is the cen-
tralization of power. Originally, the denomination
was set up to be a loose fellowship of independent
churches. Early doctrinal disputes, such as "the
new issue, set forth the trend toward centraliza-
tion. However, it was a desire for pragmatic effi-
ciency that led to the formation of a large bureau-
cracy. In recent years, a serious attempt has been
made to co-ordinate these agencies to make them more
functional.

In addition to documenting these two trends, Menzies
has provided many insights into major issues and
emphases of the denomination during these years.
The first section of his work serves as a concise
summary of the earlier histories, and like the rest
of his work, is carefully documented. Several helpful appendices, including the denomination's statement of faith, a complete historical listing of national officers and a number of statistical charts
are included. His bibliography along with those of
Synan, Brunner, and Hollenweger offer the most complete listings of Pentecostal materials.

A popularly written non-scholarly survey which should
be mentioned is Irwin Winehouse, The Assemblies of
God (New York: Vantage Press, 1959) Another excellent documented account of the organizational
structure of the Assemblies of God is Mario G.
Hoover's unpublished M.A. thesis, "Origin and Struc-
tural Development of the Assemblies of God" (Springfield, Mo.: Missouri State, 1970) Copies of this
thesis have been made available by the author and
can be purchased through the bookstore at Central
Bible College in Springfield.

An early figure in the Assemblies of God was Aimee
Semple McPherson. She soon withdrew to form her
own denomination, the International Church of the
Four Square Gospel. McPherson received an interpretation of Ezekiel's visions of the four faces--
man, lion, ox, eagle--to mean Jesus Christ; sav-

viour, baptizer, healer, and king.[14]

The history and doctrine of this denomination is
compiled by Raymond L. Cox, The Four Square Gospel
(Los Angeles: Heritage Committee, 1969)   It can
be ordered from Four Square Publications, 1100
Glendale Blvd., Los Angeles, California, 90026. Of
interest are biographies of Aimee McPherson. L.
Thomas, The Vanishing Evangelist; the Aimee Semple
McPherson Kidnapping Affair (New York: Viking
Press, 1959) offers an unfavorable analysis of her
ministry. The best of the sympathetic accounts is
Nancy Barr Mavity, Sister Aimee (Garden City, N. Y.:
Doubleday, Duran & Co., 1931)   McPherson offers
several autobiographical accounts, which must also
be noted: This is That: Personal Experiences, Ser-
mons, and Writings of Aimee Semple McPherson (Los
Angeles: Echo Park Evangelistic Association, 1923);
In the Service of the King (New York: Boni and
Liveright, 1927); and, The Story of My Life (Los
Angeles: Echo Park Evangelistic Association, 1951)

Largely due to the scandal caused by McPherson's
kidnapping, several churches of her denomination in
Minnesota and Iowa withdrew to form the Open Bible
Evangelistic Association in 1932. This group later
merged with the Bible Standard Church of Eugene,
Oregon in 1935 to become the Open Bible Standard
Evangelistic Association.[15]

The history of this church is documented in Gotfred
S. Bruland, The Origin and Development of the Open
Bible Church in Iowa (Des Moines, Iowa: Drake University, M.A. thesis, 1945)   A concise account of
the origin is found in Kendrick's The Promise Ful-

---

14.   Moore, "Handbook of Denominations, p. 59.
      George Jeffreys, an English Pentecostal,
spells out this doctrinal statute in The Miraculous
Four Square Gospel (London: Elim Publishing Co.
1929)

15.   The Bible Standard Church originated from a
      split with Mrs. Florence Crawford, Apostolic
Faith Mission in 1919. The issues of contention at
that point were: (1) her church was the only true
church; and (2) all divorced persons who had re-
married must separate from their present companions
before they could become members of the church.

filled, pp. 164-171.

The Oneness Groups

David Reed is currently doing his Ph.D. research at
Boston University on the historical and theological
origins of the "Oneness" or "Jesus Only" movement.
Fred J Foster's Think It Not Strange, A History of
the Oneness Movement (St. Louis: Pentecostal Publishing House, 1965) and Arthur L. Clanton, United
We Stand (Hazlewood, Mo.: Pentecostal Publishing
House, 1970) are currently the most comprehensive
historical accounts available on this Movement.
Menzies, in Anointed to Serve, chapter six, "The
New Issue" pp. 106-121, gives the most authoritative
description of the movement as it stands in relation
to the Assemblies of God.[16] "The New Issue" was a
controversy regarding the doctrine of the trinity
and the significance of the name Jesus.[17] Synan,

---

16. The Movement hit the Assemblies of God the
     hardest for two reasons. First, as a denomi-
nation they were perhaps the most opposed of all
Pentecostals to strong centrality of power; thus,
they had little control over doctrinal teaching.
Secondly, the teaching hit full force only two
years after they had organized. Many of their
leaders and more than 25% of their ministers embraced the teaching.

17   The distinctive teaching of the "New Issue" is
     best expressed in the Articles of Faith of the
United Pentecostal Church, largest of the Oneness
groups:

"Nature of God"

One true God--revealed Himself as Father,
through His Son in redemption, and as the
Holy Spirit.

The one true God, the Jehovah of the Old
Testament took upon Himself the form of man,
and as son of man was born of the virgin Mary.
God was in Christ reconciling the world unto
himself.

In Him dwelleth all the fullness of the God-

in the Holiness Pentecostal Movement, in a chapter
entitled "Criticism and Controversy" pp. 141-163,
offers the perspective of a disinterested onlooker.
Brumback's Suddenly From Heaven contains a helpful
chapter on the significance of this issue to the
Assemblies of God, pp. 191-215.

When the "New Issue" failed to capture the Assemblies of God, "The Pentecostal Assemblies of the
World" was created in 1916 under the leadership of
G. T. Haywood, a black from Indianapolis. The
group remained bi-racial until 1924, when the white
ministers withdrew to form their own denomination.
Two groups merged in 1945 to form the largest Oneness body "The United Pentecostal Church." A host
of splinter groups exist. For information about
these groups see Clanton's United We Stand. It is
estimated that there are about one-half million
Oneness adherents in the United States.[18] Several
autobiographical and biographical accounts exist of
early leaders in the movement, which are worthy of
note here. These include Frank J. Ewart, The Phenomenon of Pentecost (St. Louis: Pentecostal Publishing House, 1947); Ethel E. Goss, The Winds of

---

head bodily. For it pleased the Father that
in Him should all the fulness dwell.

Therefore Jesus in His humanity was, and is
man, in His deity was, and is God. His flesh
was in the lamb or sacrifice of God, He is
the only mediator between God and man, for
there is one God, and one mediator between
God and man, the man Christ Jesus.

I am the Alpha, Omega, the beginning and
ending, saith the Lord, which is, which was,
and which is to come, the Almighty.

"The Name"

Neither is there salvation in any other, for
there is none other name under heaven given
among men, whereby we must be saved.

Moore, "Handbook of Pentecostal Denominations,
p. 156.

18. Menzies, Anointed to Serve, p. 120.

<u>God</u> (New York, 1958); Mrs. M. B. Etter, <u>Marvels and</u>
<u>Miracles: Signs and Wonders</u> (Indianapolis, 1922);
and Sam Officer, <u>Wise Master Builders and the Wheels</u>
<u>of Fortune</u> (Cleveland, Tenn.: The Jesus Church,
n.d.)

Black Pentecostalism

Today, like the era following the American Revolution and the period following the Russian Revolution in 1917, history books are being rewritten.
Black awareness has caused the Negro race to real-
ize that their contribution to American history
has been distorted, if not totally ignored.

In seeking to discover their heritage and to establish their identity, many fresh insights are being
uncovered. Inevitably in this process some myths
are being created as well.

Long ignored by Pentecostals is the role that
blacks have played in their origins and development.

The first major study of black contributions is
now under way at Vanderbilt, where Garnet Pike is
writing a case study entitled,"A Historical Study
of Black Pentecostals."

Best materials available to date include Walter J.
Hollenweger, "A Black Pentecostal Concept; A For-
gotten chapter of Black History," <u>Concept</u>, Special
Issue 30, June 1970. (Copies of this may be or-
dered c/o WCC, 150 Route de Ferney, 1211 Geneva 20,
Switzerland.)

Another article is James S. Tinney, "Black Origins
of the Pentecostal Movement," <u>Christianity Today</u>,
October 8, 1971, pp. 4-6. Finally, Vinson Synan,
<u>The Holiness Pentecostal Movement</u> includes an ex-
cellent chapter on black contributions: "The Negro
Pentecostals," pp. 165-184.

There is little written on individual black denominations. Moore's <u>"Handbook of Pentecostal Denomi-</u>
<u>nations"</u> gives a quick sketch of the origins of the
major ones.

Mary Mason, <u>The History and Life Work of Bishop C.</u>
<u>H. Mason, Chief Apostle, and his Co-laborers</u> (Mem-
phis, n.p. 1934) gives background pertaining to

the Church of God in Christ, the largest black Pentecostal denomination.

Another early black Pentecostal group is documented by H. L. Fisher, History of the United Holy Church of America (n.p. n.d.). Like the Church of God in Christ, this group has holiness origins.

The Latter Rain Movement

Among the strongest critics of the Pentecostal Movement at its beginning were the older Holiness denominations and the fundamentalists. The fundamentalists charged that all signs and wonders ceased with the Apostles; therefore, such things as "speaking in other tongues" in the twentieth century were dispensationally impossible. The Pentecostals took this charge seriously, and sought to answer their critics in two ways. First, they appealed to church history. finding various individuals and groups to have experienced "tongues" from time to time throughout the centuries. A second argument was based on what came to be known as the Latter Rain Covenant.[19] This doctrine taught that Joel's prophecy "In the last days I will pour out my Spirit upon all flesh..." had been but partially fulfilled on the Day of Pentecost (Acts 2:16-20) and was to be completed just before Christ's return. Thus, the fact that the Pentecostal revival had occured implied that Christ's second advent was at hand. The fundamentalists were right in saying that supernatural miracles had largely ceased with the first century apostles; but a revival of this should now be expected.

A work that gave great influence to this teaching was David Wesley Myland, The Latter Rain Covenant and Pentecostal Power (Chicago: Evangel Publishing House, 1910) Myland actually used charts of rainfall in Palestine from 1861-1901 to show that rain was increasing in that land. From this data, he concluded that the second coming would occur shortly after 1906.[20]

---

19. J. Roswell Flower, "History of the Assemblies of God," pp. 5-6.

20. Synan, Holiness-Pentecostal Movement, p. 146.

This theme was picked up in the late forties by the "New Order of the Latter Rain." Centers of this movement were located at Bethesda Missionary Temple in Detroit, Michigan, pastored by Myrtle Beall, and at Wings of Healing Temple in Port. nd, Oregon, pastored by Dr. Thomas Wyatt. Israel's establishment as a nation in 1948 was tied to this revival, giving the Latter Rain Movement a great eschatological hope.

Patricia D. Gruits, daughter of Mrs. M. D. Beall, pastor of the Detroit Center gives a theological presentation of this basic belief in Understanding God (Detroit: The Evangel Press, 1962)

Perhaps a sidelight may here be mentioned. This movement has taken seriously Paul's declaration that in Christ there is neither Jew nor Greek, bond nor free, male nor female. Blacks and women both have found responsible roles in the power structure, and unity of spirit is a dynamic reality.

Menzies, Anointed to Serve, pp. 321-325, relates the effect of the movement on the Assemblies of God. Though the two main churches remain strong, the influence of the movement upon Pentecostalism began to wane by the mid-fifties.

Salvationist-Healing Movement

A host of independent, Pentecostal evangelists became prominent during the fifties; although they remained largely outside the Pentecostal denominational structures, they drew their base support from within the Pentecostal denominational ranks. The emphases of their ministries were mass evangelism, divine healing, and deliverance. The impact of these men on the Assemblies of God is documented by Menzies, Anointed to Serve, pp. 330-335.

Best known and most successful of these men is Oral Roberts. In his recent autobiography, The Call (New York: Doubleday & Co., 1972), Roberts describes his ministry as one that set the stage for the rise of the charismatic movement (p. 129) In time his audience gradually drew in more people from main-line denominations. Thus, when the charismatic movement began its sweep in the early sixties, a large number of people had already been

oriented to its message. It was a logical conclu-
sion for Roberts, therefore, to leave the Pentecostal Holiness Church and join the United Methodist
Church in 1968, and seek to establish himself within
the mainstream of historic Christianity.

Several loose evangelistic affiliations have been in
existence at one time or another. The best known
of these was started by Gordon Lindsay, with headquarters in Dallas, Texas. Through his magazine,
The Voice of Healing, the association gained great
influence among many Pentecostals. His autobiography, The Gordon Lindsay Story (Dallas: The Voice
of Healing Publishing Co., n.d.) and biography,
William Branham, a Man Sent From God (Jefferson-
ville, Ind.: William Branham, 1950) portray the
mission he sought to accomplish. Other men who
associated with the Voice of Healing at one time
or another include Jack Coe, T. L. Osborn, M. A.
Daoud, W. V. Grant, and William Caldwell. The organization was revived in 1967 under the name
"Christ for the Nations."

Another famous controversial tent evangelist of the
era was A. A. Allen. His autobiography, Born to
Lose, Bound to Win (Garden City. N. Y.: Doubleday
& Co., 1970), provides an interesting account of his
ministry.

Carrying on the tradition of Aimee Semple McPherson
in the present day has been Kathryn Kuhlman. Her
two books, I Believe in Miracles (Englewood Cliffs,
N. J.: Prentice-Hall, Inc., 1962) and God Can Do It
Again (Englewood Cliffs, N. J.: Prentice-Hall, Inc.,
1968) are largely autobiographical. A slightly
more controversial book, Alan Spraggett, Kathryn
Kuhlman, the Woman Who Believes in Miracles (New
York: The World Publishing Co. 1970), assesses her
ministry in light of the growing trend of "divine
healers" of her day.

Charismatic Movement

Michael Harper, an Englishman, has written the best
account tracing the development of the Charismatic
Revival in main-line denominations: As at the Beginning: the Twentieth Century Pentecostal Revival (London: Hodder and Stoughton, 1965) A close second
is John L. Sherrill, They Speak with Other Tongues
(New York: McGraw-Hill Book Co., 1964) In both
cases the modern revival is set in the context of

classical Pentecostalism. So much has happened in
the Movement since these works have been written,
however, that they cannot be an adequate guide to
the Movement as it now stands.

David J. du Plessis, a former Assemblies of God
minister from South Africa, is generally cited for
introducing Pentecostalism to the mainline denominations. As a long-time Executive Secretary for
the World Pentecostal Conference, du Plessis was in
a unique position to contact leaders in the World
Council of Churches. He also was the only official
Pentecostal observer at the Second Vatican Council,
and has since played a large role in the developing
Pentecostal Movement among Roman Catholics. His
autobiographical The Spirit Bade Me Go: the Astound-
ing Move of God in the Denominational Churches (Oakland, California: David J du Plessis, 1960) has
undergone several revisions and reprintings, and is
still available through the author (David J. du
Plessis, 3742 Linwood Avenue, Oakland, California,
94602)

Dennis J Bennett, Nine O'clock in the Morning
(Plainfield, N. J.: Logos Press, 1970) is the account of an Anglican who early became involved in
the Charismatic Revival. Bennett later teamed with
his wife, Rita, to write The Holy Spirit and You
(Plainfield, N. J.: Logos Press, 1971) a work that
has proved helpful to orient people from other
theological traditions to the Pentecostal experience. An important influence in the beginnings of
this movement was Trinity Magazine (no longer published) edited by Jean Stone, a member of Bennett's parish in Van Nuys, California.

A host of other books is available; these merely
serve to set the others in historical perspective.

The Catholic Pentecostals

J. Gordon Melton, The Catholic Pentecostal Movement
(Evanston, Ill.: Garrett Theological Seminary. Nov.
1971) provides the basic bibliography for this section of the Charismatic Movement. Copies are available from the seminary.

Several books on Catholic Pentecostals are well
worth mentioning here. The first to appear was
Kevin and Dorothy Ranaghan, Catholic Pentecostals
(Paramus, N. J.: Paulist Press, 1969) It is an

excellent historical account of the development of the movement among Catholics. The others: Edward D. O'Connor, The Pentecostal Movement in the Catholic Church (Notre Dame, Ave Maria Press, 1971); Donald L. Gelpi, Pentecostalism: A Theological Viewpoint (New York, Paulist Press, 1971); and two books by J. Massingberd Ford, The Pentecostal Experience, a New Direction for American Catholics (New York: Paulist Press, 1970), and Baptism of the Spirit: Three Essays on the Pentecostal Experience (Techny. Ill.: Divine Word Publications, 1971), are all attempts to interpret the Pentecostal experience in light of traditional Roman Catholic theology.

Kilian McDonnell, Executive Director of the Institute for Ecumenical and Cultural Research, Collegeville, Minnesota, presents the best. analysis of what has been happening in a brief essay Catholic Pentecostalism: Problems in Evaluation (Pecos, New Mexico: Dove Publications, 1970), a reprint that originally appeared in Dialog, Winter 1970. McDonnell is seeking to establish his Institute as the center for future Catholic Pentecostal studies.

The Jesus Movement

Like the rise of classic Pentecostalism, the Jesus Movement of the late 1960's stands outside the mainstream of organized Christianity. A host of descriptive books is coming off the press. At this point in history it is impossible to assess the impact of the Movement, or to predict in what direction it is heading. Ronald M. Enroth, et al, The Jesus People (Grand Rapids: Eerdmans, 1972) to date is the most comprehensive chronicle of the Movement. William S. Cannon, The Jesus Revolution (Nashville: Broadman Press, 1971) is an attempt to assess the Movement in light of evangelical theology. Jess Moody, The Jesus Freaks (Waco, Texas: Word, 1971) includes a helpful list of communities throughout the United States. Most of the books take the form of chronicle accounts of the Movement. These books include John A. MacDonald, The House of Acts (Carol Stream, Ill.: Creation House, 1970), Duane Pederson, Jesus People (Glendale, Calif.: Regal Books, 1971) Pat King, The Jesus People Are Coming (Plainfield, N. J.: Logos Press, 1971), Lowell D. Streiker, The Jesus Trip: Advent of the Jesus Freaks (Nashville: Abingdon Press, 1971), Edward Plowman, The Jesus Movement in America (Cool, 1971) Arthur Blessitt, Turned on to Jesus (Haw-

thorn, 1971), and Roger C. Palms, The Jesus Kids
(Valley Forge, Pa.: Judson Press, 1971)   Chris-
tianity Today has printed many articles on the
Jesus Movement.   These have been compiled in A News
Diary of the Jesus Movement (n.p., 1971)

THEOLOGICAL DISTINCTIVES

A Pentecostal Theology has never actually been
written.   Three early attempts, Myer Pearlman,
Knowing the Doctrines of the Bible (Springfield:
Gospel Publishing House, 1937), Ernest S. Williams,
Systematic Theology, 3 Vols. (Springfield, Gospel
Publishing House, 1953)   and P. C. Nelson, Bible
Doctrines; A Handbook on Pentecostal Theology (Enid,
Oklahoma: South Western Press, 1936) were based
largely on existing non-Pentecostal works and were
designed to provide a basic structure in theology
for a large number of clergy who had not had the
opportunity of formal training.   Carl Brumback
What Meaneth This (Springfield, Mo.: Gospel Publishing House, 1947) perhaps is the best apology
for the Pentecostal distinctives.

To date most Pentecostal Bible Colleges are using
theologies written for other traditions in the
training of their ministers.

The Pentecostal Holiness Church is publishing annually the "King Memorial Lecture Series."   This is
the most recent expression of Holiness-Pentecostal
theology.   The series includes: J. A. Synan, Christian Life in Depth, 1964; H. P. Robinson, Redemption
Conceived and Revealed, 1965; B. E. Underwood, The
Gifts of the Spirit, 1967; Noel Brooks; Scriptural
Holiness, 1967; J. A. Synan, The Shape of Things to
Come, 1969; and B. E. Underwood, The Spirit's Sword,
1969.   All are published by Advocate Press in
Franklin Springs, Georgia.

The Holy Spirit

The largest emphasis, of course, is on the work of
the Holy Spirit.   Here the most recent books in the
field are written by non-Pentecostals.   Frederick
Dale Bruner, A Theology of the Holy Spirit, the
Pentecostal Experience and the New Testament Witness
(Grand Rapids: Eerdmans, 1970), and James D. G. Dunn,
Baptism in the Holy Spirit: a Reexamination of the
New Testament Teaching of the Gift of the Spirit in

Relation to Pentecostalism Today (Naperville, Ill.:
Allenson, 1970) Dunn's work is largely a Biblical
study while Bruner divides his work in two sections,
dealing first with the Pentecostal understanding of
the doctrine as it developed historically, then
moving in to consider the Biblical evidence. Bruner
includes a helpful appendix of documents upon which
the Pentecostal doctrine of the Holy Spirit is based.
He also provides a short informative bibliographical
essay on the existing works that are relevant to his
book, and finally his extensive bibliography is
worthy of note.

No one Pentecostal theologian has gained wider acceptance among the Pentecostal denominations than
the Englishman, Donald Gee. The Ministry Gifts of
Christ (Springfield: Gospel Publishing House, 1930)
Concerning Spiritual Gifts (Springfield: Gospel Publishing House, 1937) and Spiritual Gifts in the
Work of the Ministry Today (Springfield: Gospel Pub-
lishing House, 1963) are probably his best known
writings on the work of the Holy Spirit. The influ-
ence of other writers has been limited primarily to
their own denominations. These include Harold
Horton, The Gifts of the Spirit (Luten, England:
Redemption Tidings Bookroom, 1934) and The Baptism
of the Holy Spirit (London: Victory Press, 1956),
Ralph M. Riggs, The Spirit Himself (Springfield:
Gospel Publishing House, 1949), Myer Pearlman, The
Heavenly Gift: Studies in the Work of the Holy
Spirit (Springfield: Gospel Publishing House, 1935)
Aimee Semple McPherson, The Baptism of the Holy
Spirit (Los Angeles: Four Square Gospel, 1928)
George Jeffreys, Pentecostal Rays: The Baptism and
the Gifts of the Spirit (Minneapolis: Northern Gos-
pel Publishing House, 1946), Melvin L. Hodges,
Spiritual Gifts (Springfield: Gospel Publishing
House, 1964), W. H. Turner, The Difference Between
Regeneration, Sanctification and the Pentecostal
Baptism (Franklin Springs, Ga.: Publishing House of
the Pentecostal Holiness Church, 1947) J. H. King,
From Passover to Pentecost (Franklin Springs, Ga.:
Publishing House of the Pentecostal Holiness Church,
1914) and Bennie S. Triplett, A Contemporary Study
of the Holy Spirit (Cleveland, Tenn.: Pathway Press,
1970)

Frank J. Ewart, The Revelation of Jesus Christ (St.
Louis: Pentecostal Publishing House, n.d.) provides
the best theological defense for the "Oneness" doctrine. The teaching is refuted in Carl Brumback,
God in Three Persons (Cleveland, Tenn.: Pathway

Press, 1959)

The early Pentecostals drew heavily on prominent
Holiness leaders of the late nineteenth century and
early twentieth century in formulating their the-
ology of the Holy Spirit. Representative titles
of this era include R. A. Torrey, The Holy Spirit
(Westwood, N. J.: Fleming H. Revell Co., 1927)
Andrew Murray, The Full Blessing of Pentecost
(Westwood, N. J.: Fleming H. Revell Co., 1908), A.
J. Gordon, The Ministry of the Spirit (New York:
Fleming H. Revell, 1894) A. B. Simpson, The Holy
Spirit, 2 Vols. (Harrisburg, Pa.: Christian Publi-
cations Inc., n.d.), and Charles G. Finney, Power
from on High (London: Victory Press, 1944)

Glossolalia

From the outset, the Pentecostal teaching which met
the most controvery has been the association of
glossolalia with the baptism in the Holy Spirit.
The most exhaustive study of this phenomenon is
Lincoln M. Vivier's unpublished M.D. thesis,
"Glossolalia" (Johannesburg: University of Wit-
watersrand, 1960) Vivier studies the Biblical
evidence and the historical occurrence of tongues
before the twentieth century He then considers a
host of case studies, and concludes that Pentecostals tend to be slightly above average in their
psychological adjustment. The best overview from a
Pentecostal perspective is Wade Horton, ed., The
Glossolalia Phenomenon (Cleveland, Tenn.: Pathway
Press, 1966) a compilation of articles by prominent Pentecostals. It treats the phenomenon in its
historical and theological aspects. The classic
Biblical exegesis from a Pentecostal point of view
is William G. MacDonald, Glossolalia in the New
Testament (Springfield, Mo.: Gospel Publishing House,
1964) a reprint of an article first appearing in
the Evangelical Theological Society Bulletin
7:59-68, Spring, 1964.[21] A significant early work

---

21. An excellent supplement to this is Anthony
     Palma "Tongues and Prophecy: a Comparative
Study in Charismata" (St. Louis: Concordia Theological Seminary, 1966), an unpublished S.T.M. dissertation. Palma's analysis brings him to the con-
clusion that the purpose of glossolalia is praise.

is Robert C. Dalton, Tongues Like as of Fire: a
Critical Study of Modern Tongues Movements in the
Light of Apostolic and Patristic Times (Springfield,
Mo.: Gospel Publishing House, 1945)

As glossolalia became prominent in mainline denominations, church leaders were at a loss as to how to
handle the situation. The first official response
in the Protestant Episcopal Church was a Pastoral
Letter Regarding Speaking in Tongues by the late
Bishop James A. Pike of California. The text of
this letter appeared in Pastoral Psychology 15:
56-61, May 1964. A second official pronouncement is
a Report on Glossolalia (Minneapolis, Minn.: Commission of Evangelism of the American Lutheran Church,
1964) A third is the Report of the Special Committee on the Work of the Holy Spirit (Philadelphia:
United Presbyterian Church of the U.S.A. 1970)

All are efforts to give guidance to all parties con-
cerned when glossolalia appears in the local church.

A host of psychological and theological studies have
been written on glossolalia. Most recent is John P.
Kildahl, The Psychology of Speaking in Tongues (New
York: Harper & Row, 1972) Dr. Kildahl, on the
faculty at the New York Post Graduate Center for
Mental Health, and a member of the investigating
commission for the American Lutheran Church, has
spent over ten years studying glossolalia. He offers a sympathetic ear to those who participate in
the phenomenon, but concludes that, if speaking in
tongues is to be understood as a gift of the Spirit,
it must be in terms of how it is used, not by the
mere fact that it occurs.

Helpful in Kildahl's work is an anlysis of several
of the leading monographs that have been written in
the field. Morton T. Kelsey, Tongues Speaking: An
Experiment in Spiritual Experience (Garden City, N.
Y.: Doubleday & Co., 1964), George Barton Cutten,
Speaking with Tongues, Historically and Psychologi-
cally Considered (New Haven, Conn.: Yale University
Press, 1927) Ira J. Martin, Glossolalia in the Apostolic Church; A Survey Study of Tongues Speech (Berea, Ky.: Berea College, 1960) Wayne E. Oates and
others, Glossolalia Tongue Speaking in Biblical,
Historical and Psychological Perspective (Nashville:
Abingdon Press, 1967), all treat the glossolalia
phenomenon primarily from a psychological point of
view. Also to be noted at this point is a significant article, James N. Lapsley and John H. Simpson,

"Speaking in Tongues: Token of Group Acceptance and
Divine Approval," Pastoral Psychology, XV (May 1964)
48-53, and "Speaking in Tongues: Infantile Babble,"
Pastoral Psychology, XV (September 1964), 16-24.
Each of these works is written by outside observers,
whose attitudes toward the experience range from
sympathy to hostility. William J. Samarin, Tongues
of Men and Angels (New York: Macmillan, 1972) is
perhaps the best linguistic study of the glossolalia
phenomenon.

An account of an investigator who became personally
involved in the experience is John L. Sherrill, They
Speak with Other Tongues (New York: McGraw-Hill,
1964). A similar account of an earlier investiga-
tion is Elmer C. Miller, Pentecost Examined by a
Baptist Lawyer (Springfield, Mo.: Gospel Publishing
House, 1936)

Works critical of the present phenomenon from a
theological viewpoint include Robert G. Gromacki,
The Modern Tongues Movement (Philadelphia: Presby-
terian and Reformed Publishing Co., 1967), Anthony
A. Hoekema, What About Tongue-Speaking? (Grand
Rapids: Eerdmans Publishing Co. 1966) Donald W.
Burdick, Tongues: To Speak or Not To Speak (Chicago:
Moody Press, 1969), Donald S. Metz, Speaking in
Tongues: An Analysis (Kansas City. Mo.: Nazarene
Publishing House, 1964) and H. J Stolee, Speaking
in Tongues (Minneapolis: Augsburg Publishing House,
1963) A positive presentation is by a Lutheran
Laurence Christenson, Speaking in Tongues and its
Significance for the Church (Minneapolis: Bethany
Fellowship, 1968) W. H. Turner, Pentecost and
Tongues (Franklin Springs, Ga.: Advocate Press,
1968) supplies the latest thinking among classic
Pentecostals on the issue.

Divine Healing

A third emphasis in the Pentecostal Movement has
been divine healing. This emphasis received its
impetus from the leader of the Christian and Missionary Alliance, A. B. Simpson. Simpson's views
on healing are best expressed in his book, The
Gospel of Healing (New York: Christian Alliance
Publishing Co., 1915) Also influential was Smith
Wigglesworth, Ever Increasing Faith (Springfield,
Mo.: Gospel Publishing House, 1924) and A. J. Gordon, The Ministry of Healing or, Miracles of Cure
in All Ages (New York: Revell, 1882) This was

reprinted in 1961 by Christian Publications, Harrisburg, Pennsylvania. F. F. Bosworth, Christ the Healer (Racine, Wis.: n.p., 1927) defended the position: faith is always rewarded with healing. This position influenced thousands of Pentecostals for years.

Donald Gee, Concerning Spiritual Gifts (Springfield, Mo.: Gospel Publishing House, n.d.) and George Jeffreys, Healing Rays (London: Henry E. Walter, Ltd., 1952) are standard works.[22]

The more prolific writers on divine healing have quite naturally been the faith evangelists who gained popularity during the fifties and early sixties. The best of these are T. L. Osborn, Healing the Sick and Casting Out Devils (Tulsa: T. L. Osborn Evangelistic Association, 1955) and Oral Roberts, If You Need Healing, Do These Things (Tulsa: Oral Roberts, 1947) Roberts' work went through several editions and has been revised considerably each time. Other examples of this literature include Gordon Lindsay, World Evangelism Now by Healing and Miracles (Glendale, California: Church Press, 1951); William Caldwell, Meet the Healer (Tulsa: Miracle Moments Evangelistic Association, Inc., 1965); A. A. Allen, God's Guarantee to Heal You (Dallas: A. A. Allen, 1950); W. V. Grant, Divine Healing Answers, 2 Vols. (Waxahachie, Texas: Southwestern Bible Institute Press, 1952); Tommy Hicks, Manifest Deliverance for You Now (Lancaster, California: Tommy Hicks, 1952); Theodore Fitch, Our Afflictions: Cause and Remedy (Council Bluffs, Iowa: Theodore Fitch, n.d.); and Thomas Wyatt, A Study in Healing and Deliverance, 2 Vols. (Los Angeles: Wings of Healing, n.d.)

For a more complete listing of the writings of these men consult the "Bibliography on Divine Healing," compiled by Juanita Raudzus, available at Oral Ro-

---

22. Gee's work in particular has had great influence among Pentecostal circles. This has been due to the Pentecostal teaching that divine healing is in the atonement: "By whose stripes we are healed" (I Peter 2:24) Gee's ministry has served as a corrective to the popular, though unofficial, idea that one without faith to experience divine healing cannot be sure of his salvation either.

berts University for $1.00.

Though the faith evangelists have taken the lead in
this area, the Pentecostal denominations have also
produced a number of titles worthy of note. These
works include James A. Cross, Healing in the Church
(Cleveland, Tenn.: Pathway Press, 1962); Hart R.
Armstrong, Divine Healing, 2 Vols. (Springfield,
Mo.: Gospel Publishing House, 1948); William H.
Turner, Christ the Great Physician (Franklin Springs,
Ga.: Advocate Press, 1941); Noel Brooks, Sickness,
Health and God (Franklin Springs, Ga.: Advocate
Press, n.d.); and Gordon F. Atter, The Student's
Handbook on Divine Healing (Peterborough, Ontario:
The Book Nook, 1960)

Women have played a prominent role in the Healing
ministry of the Pentecostal Movement. Aimee Semple
McPherson's teaching is illustrated in her Divine
Healing Sermons (Los Angeles: International Church
of the Four Square Gospel, n.d.) Kathryn Kuhlman,
I Believe in Miracles (Englewood Cliffs, N. J.:
Prentice Hall, Inc., 1962) and God Can Do It Again
(Englewood Cliffs, N. J.: Prentice Hall, Inc. 1969
are contemporary expressions of the impact of the
Divine Healing teaching. The chief proponent of
the "Healing of the Memories" concept, Agnes Sanford, has published several works of note. Best
known is The Healing Light (St. Paul, Minn.: Macalester Park Publishing Co., 1947) Other of her
writings include Behold Your God (St. Paul, Minn.:
Macalester Park Publishing Co., 1958), The Healing
Gifts of the Spirit (Philadelphia: J B. Lippincott
Co., 1966), and The Healing Power of the Bible
(Philadelphia: J. B. Lippincott Co., 1969) Also
worthy of mention is Anne S. White, Healing Adven-
ture (London: Arthur Janes, Ltd. 1969) and Day-
spring (Plainfield, N. J.: Logos Press, 1972) Mrs.
White is one of Sanford's best known disciples, and
is considered by many to be her successor.

A helpful analysis of the whole healing phenomenon
is George Bishop, Faith Healing: God or Fraud?
(Los Angeles: Sherbourne Press, Inc., 1967) A
final work on healing should be noted, Gilbert W.
Kirby. The Question of Healing; Some Thoughts on
Healing and Suffering (London: Victory Press, 1967)
This work is a collection of articles by men repre-
sentative of most branches of the Christian Faith.
One is enabled to view the Pentecostal position on
Divine Healing in light of the teaching of the
whole church.

Special Issues

The "Deliverance Ministry" (exorcism or the casting out of demons) has long played a role in Pentecostal circles. Oral Roberts, Deliverance from Fear and From Sickness (Tulsa: Oral Roberts, 1954) represents the early teaching on the subject. The doctrine was developed through the faith evangelists associated with The Voice of Healing. The teaching and practice are now being expressed in the Charismatic Movement, largely through the influence of the Holy Spirit Teaching Mission of Fort Lauderdale, Florida. Leaders Derek Prince, Bob Mumford, Charles Simpson and Don Basham's writings appear in the periodical New Wine, and less frequently in the Logos Journal.

Prophecy has been another interest of Pentecostals from their beginnings. Frank M. Boyd, long-time Assemblies of God Bible school teacher, has been the guiding influence of this interest. Ages and Dispensations (Springfield, Mo.: Gospel Publishing House, 1949) and Introduction to Prophecy (Springfield, Mo.: Gospel Publishing House, 1948) are his best known works. In addition to these, he has published several commentaries on the Old Testament prophets.

Donald N. Bowdle has just written a perceptive study of regeneration as preparatory to the baptism with the Holy Spirit: Redemption Accomplished and Applied: a Study in the Doctrine of Salvation (Cleveland, Tenn.: Pathway Press, 1972)

William G. MacDonald has offered a Pentecostal concept of the doctrine of the Church, "A People in Community: Theological Interpretation,' which appears in a book edited by James L. Garrett, The Concept of the Believers' Church (Scottdale, Pa.: Herald Press, 1969, pp. 143-164) based on the papers delivered in Louisville, Kentucky at the 1967 conference on the concept of the Believers' Church. MacDonald stands with Dietrich Bonhoeffer, The Communion of Saints; a Dogmatic Inquiry into the Sociology of the Church (New York: Harper and Row, 1963) and against Ernest Troeltsch, in arguing that the Church is a community of faith, rather than a society.

A sociological study of Pentecostalism which must be noted is William W. Wood, Culture and Personality; Aspects of the Pentecostal Holiness Religion (The

Hague: Mouton Co., 1965)

MISSIONS

Another major emphasis of Pentecostals has been
missions. Walter J Hollenweger, The Pentecostals,
as one would expect, gives the most comprehensive
coverage of the impact Pentecostals have made
throughout the world. Charles W. Conn, Where the
Saints Have Trod; a History of Church of God Missions (Cleveland, Tenn.: Pathway Press, 1959)
Serena M. Hodges, Look on the Fields; a Missionary
Survey (Springfield, Mo.: Gospel Publishing House,
1963) and Noel Perkin and John Garlock, Our World
Witness (Springfield, Mo.: Gospel Publishing House,
1965) represent the best denominational sources
available.

Lester F. Sumrall, Through Blood and Fire in Latin
America (Grand Rapids: Zondervan, 1944) and Christian Lalive D'Epiney, Haven of the Masses; a Study
of the Pentecostal Movement in Chile (London: Lut-
terworth Press, 1969) are exemplary of literature
written on particular areas. Steve Durasoff, The
Russian Protestants (Cranbury, N. J.: Associated
University Press, 1969) contains three chapters on
the Russian Pentecostals which provide a rare insight of what is going on behind the Iron Curtain.

Melvin L. Hodges, The Indigenous Church (Springfield, Mo.: Gospel Publishing House, 1953) spells
out the Pentecostal philosophy of missions. Hodges
argues much like Donald A. McGavran, Understanding
Church Growth (Grand Rapids: Eerdmans, 1970), break-
ing away from the compound concept of Christian
world missions.

Two representative biographies of Pentecostal missions are Lester Sumrall, Lillian Trasher; Nile
Mother (Springfield, Mo.: Gospel Publishing House,
1951) and Angeline Tucker, He is in Heaven (New
York: McGraw Hill Book Co., 1965) Miss Trasher
broke her engagement with her fiancee to run an or-
phanage in Egypt, while Jay Tucker became a martyr
during the Congo civil war in the mid-sixties.

HOMILETICS AND SERMONS

Two books on preaching best representing Pentecostal efforts are Guy P. Duffield, Pentecostal Preach-

ing (New York: Vantage Press, 1957) and C. L. Allen,
Pentecostal Preaching is Different (Los Angeles: B.
N. Robertson, 1961)   Both developed out of an an-
nual lectureship series on preaching held at L.I.F.E.
Bible College.[23]   H. P. Robinson   Heaven's Quest
for a Man Like God (Franklin Springs, Ga.: Advocate
Press, 1969) also offers insights in preaching from
a Pentecostal perspective.

The best known sermon collection in Pentecostal
ranks is C. M. Ward, Revivaltime Sermons (Springfield, Mo.: Gospel Publishing House, 1953-) based
on his weekly radio broadcasts. The Pentecostal
Pulpit (Springfield, Mo.: Gospel Publishing House),
an earlier series published by the Assemblies of God,
should also be mentioned here.

Most of the titles mentioned in the theology section
are published sermons. In addition to these, im-
portant representative early works include N. J
Holmes, Life Sketches and Sermons (Royston, Ga.:
Press of the Pentecostal Holiness Church, 1920)
Robert L. Parham, comp., Selected Sermons of the
Late Charles F. Parham and Sarah E. Parham (Joplin,
Mo.: Robert L. Parham, 1941), F. M. Britton, Pentecostal Truth; or Sermons on Regeneration, Sanctification, the Baptism of the Holy Spirit, Divine Healing, the Second Coming of Jesus, etc. (Royston, Ga.:
Publishing House of the Pentecostal Holiness Church,
1919) J. H. King, Christ, God's Love Gift (Franklin
Springs, Ga.: Advocate Press, 1969), and G. F. Tay-
lor, The Second Coming (Franklin Springs, Ga.: Advocate Press, 1950)

APOLOGETICS

Several books have been written to set forth Pen-
tecostal belief and practice to the non-Pentecostal
world. The Church of God (Cleveland, Tennessee)
has produced by far the greatest number: Ray H.
Hughes, Church of God Distinctives (Cleveland, Tenn.:
Pathway Press, 1968) What is Pentecost? (Cleveland,
Tenn.: Pathway Press, 1963), Earl P Paulk, Your
Pentecostal Neighbor (Cleveland, Tenn.: Pathway
Press, 1958), and Frank W. Lemons, Our Pentecostal

---

23.   L.I.F.E. is the Bible College of the Inter-
      national Church of the Four Square Gospel.

<u>Heritage</u> (Cleveland, Tenn.: Pathway Press, 1961)

Other works include M. A. Tomlinson, <u>Basic Bible Beliefs</u> (Cleveland, Tenn.: White Wing Publishing House, 1961), and United Pentecostal Church, <u>What We Believe and Teach</u> (St. Louis: Pentecostal Publishing House, n.d.)

Though always careful to maintain their distinctives, Pentecostals have felt a growing affinity with Evangelical Christianity. One tangible result of this has been Russell P. Spittler's book <u>Cults and Isms; Twenty Alternatives to Evangelical Christianity</u> (Grand Rapids: Baker Book House, 1962)

APPENDIX A

A List of Pentecostal Denominations

The following list of Pentecostal churches appeared in Everett L. Moore, Handbook of Pentecostal Denominations in the United States. Statistics given are taken from the 1972 edition of Yearbook of American Churches and the 5th edition [1970] of Frank Mead, Handbook of Protestant Denominations in the United States where available. Moore's figures are kept in a few cases. Obviously, some of these figures are inaccurate. However, the listing does provide the comparative size of the denominations when grouped by doctrinal distinctives.

Holiness Pentecostal Denominations:	Churches	Membership
Apostolic Faith Mission	44	4,835
Church of God (Cleveland, Tenn.)	4,024	272,276
Church of God in Christ	4,500	425,000
Church of God of Prophecy	1,561	51,527
Church of God (Mountain Assembly)	100	3,500
Church of God (World Headquarters)	2,025	75,890
Congregational Holiness Church	147	4,859
Emmanuel Holiness Church	56	1,200
Fire Baptized Holiness Church of God in America	300	6,000
International Pentecostal Assemblies	60	6,500
Original Church of God	70	20,000
Pentecostal Church of Christ	43	1,209
Pentecostal Fire Baptized Holiness Church	41	545
Pentecostal Free Will Baptists	150	13,500
Pentecostal Holiness Church	1,324	69,679
United Holy Church of America	470	28,980
TOTALS: 16 Denominations	14,915	985,500

Keswick Pentecostal Denominations:	Churches	Membership
Assemblies of God	8,734	670,000
California Evangelistic Association	50	4,000
Calvary Pentecostal Church	22	8,000
Christian Church of North America	110	10,000
Elim Missionary Assemblies	60	3,500
House of David	66	40,816
Independent Assemblies of God	136	--
International Church of the Four Square Gospel	741	89,215
Open Bible Standard Churches	275	30,000
Pentecostal Church of God of America	975	115,000
United Full Gospel Churches	50	--
United Fundamentalist Church	300	--
World Church	--	--
Zion Evangelistic Fellowship	96	10,000
TOTALS: 14 Denominations	11,615	980,531

Jesus Only (Oneness) Pentecostal Denominations:	Churches	Membership
Apostolic Church	--	--
Apostolic Overcoming Holy Church of God	300	75,000
Associated Brotherhood of Christians	40	2,500
Church of our Lord Jesus Christ of the Apostolic Faith	155	45,000
Full Salvation Union	--	--
Jesus Church	--	--
Pentecostal Assemblies of the World	550	45,000
United Pentecostal Church	2,400	250,000
TOTALS: 8 Denominations	3,445	417,500

APPENDIX B

Major Pentecostal Publishing Houses in the United States

1. Advocate Press, P.O. Box 98, Franklin Springs, Ga. 30639   (Pentecostal Holiness)
2. Congregational Holiness Publishing House, Griffin, Ga. 30223
3. Echo Park Evangelistic Association, 1100 Glendale Blvd. Los Angeles, California   90026   (International Church of the Four Square Gospel)
4. Gospel Publishing House, 1445 Boonville Ave.   Springfield, Mo.   65802   (Assemblies of God)
5. Logos International, 185 N. Ave.   Plainfield, N.J. 07060   (Independent)
6. Pathway Press, 1080 Montgomery Ave., Cleveland, Tenn. 37311   (Church of God, Cleveland, Tenn.)
7. Pentecostal Publishing House, 3645 S. Grand Blvd., St. Louis, Mo.   63418   (United Pentecostal Church)
8. Voice of Healing Publishing Co., P.O. Box 8658, Dallas, Texas   75216   (Christ for the Nations)
9. White Wing Publishing House, Keith St., Cleveland, Tenn.   37311   (Church of God of Prophecy)

APPENDIX C

Pentecostal Periodicals

Vinson Synan suggests that the Pentecostal Movement was
spread worldwide largely due to the wide spread coverage
it received in the Holiness Periodicals.[24]

The following lists suggest the Pentecostals have learned
the importance of periodical literature as an avenue for
perpetuating their heritage.

A more extensive listing of Pentecostal Periodicals,
Juanita Walker, A Bibliography of the Pentecostal Periodical Holdings in the Oral Roberts University Collection,
(Tulsa, Oklahoma: Oral Roberts University) can be ob-
tained from the university for $3.00. Walker's bibliogra-
phy takes the format of Ulrich's International Periodical
Directory listing addresses, frequency of publication and
subscription rates where relevant. No effort has been
made to include inclusive dates of ORU's holdings.

I Early Pentecostal Periodicals[25]

*1. The Apostolic Faith. Bi-monthly. edited by Charles
   F. Parham; later by E. N. Bell.
*2. Apostolic Faith. Los Angeles. William J. Seymour,
   editor.
*3. Apostolic Faith. Portland, Oregon. Florence Craw-
   ford, editor.
*4. Apostolic Messenger. Toronto, Canada. A. H. Argue.
*5. The Christian Evangel. J. Roswell Flower, editor.
   Plainfield, Ind. Weekly.
*6. Latter Rain Evangel. William H. Piper, pastor of the
   Stone Church in Chicago. Monthly.
*7. Pentecostal Testimony. William Durham, editor.
*8. Sampson's Foxes. A. J. Tomlinson. Monthly.
*9. Tried by Fire. Topeka, Kansas. Herbert & Lillie
   Buffum. Monthly.
*10. Word and Witness. Melvern, Arkansas. Edited by.
   M. M. Pinson; later E. N. Bell. 1913-1916.

II Official Organs of Classic Pentecostal Denominations

1. Advocate, Advocate Press, Pentecostal Holiness, P.O.
   Box 98, Franklin Springs, Ga. 30639, bi-weekly. $2.00.
2. Bridegroom's Messenger, International Pentecostal Assemblies, 892 Berne St. S. E. Atlanta, Ga. 30316, monthly.

---

24. Vinson Synan, The Relationship of the Holiness Move-
    ment to the Pentecostal Movement (Wilmore, Ky.: As-
    bury Theological Seminary, May 2, 1972, p. 4, unpublished
    lecture)
25. *Periodical has ceased publication.

APPENDIX C   (continued)

3. Calvary Tidings, Calvary Pentecostal Church, Olympia, Washington. Monthly.
4. The Church of God, Church of God World Headquarters, 9305 224th St., Queens Village, New York, 11428, bi-monthly $1.50.
5. Church of God Evangel, Pathway Press, 1080 Montgomery Ave., Cleveland, Tenn., 37311, bi-monthly. $3.00.
6. Elim Pentecostal Herald, Elim Missionary Assemblies, Lima, New York. Monthly.
7. Four Square World Advance, International Church of the Four Square Gospel, 1100 Glendale Blvd. Los Angeles, Cal., 90026, monthly. Formerly Foursquare Magazine until 1964.
8. Gospel Herald, Church of God of the Mountain Assembly, Jellico, Tenn. monthly. $1.50.
9. Gospel Messenger, Congregational Holiness Church, Box 290, Griffin, Ga., 30223, monthly. $1.50.
10. Harvest Time, United Pentecostal Church, Inc. 3645 S. Grand Blvd., St. Louis, Mo., 63118.
11. Herald of Faith, Independent Assemblies of God, San Diego, Cal., monthly.
12. The Herald, Church of God of Apostolic Faith, 2200 W. Edison, Tulsa, Oklahoma, 74103. Ceased publication May 1966.
13. Light of Hope, The Apostolic Faith, N. W. and Burnside, Portland, Ore., 97209, bi-monthly. Formerly The Apostolic Faith to 1966.
14. Light of the World, The Jesus Church, Box 652, Cleveland, Tenn., 37311, quarterly. $2.00.
15. Message of the Open Bible, Open Bible Standard Churches, 1159 24th St., Des Moines, Iowa, 50311, bi-monthly. $2.00.
16. The Messenger, (Original) Church of God, Chattanooga, Tenn. Semi-monthly.
17. The Pentecostal Evangel, Gospel Publishing House, Assemblies of God, 1445 Boonville Ave., Springfield, Mo., 65802, weekly. $4.00.
18. Pentecostal Free-Will Baptist Messenger, Pentecostal Free-Will Baptist Messenger, Box 966, Dunn, N. C. Monthly. $2.00.
19. Pentecostal Herald, United Pentecostal Church, 3645 S. Grand Blvd., St. Louis, Mo., 63418, monthly. $2.00.
20. Pentecostal Messenger, Pentecostal Church of America, Box 850, Joplin, Mo., 64801, monthly. $2.00.
21. White Wing Messenger, White Wing Publishing House, Cleveland, Tenn., 37311, weekly. $2.50.
22. Wings of Truth, Church of God of Prophecy, Box 5535, Roanoke, Va., 24012, monthly. $1.50.

APPENDIX C   (continued)

III   Periodicals of Salvationist-Faith Healing Evangelists

1. Abundant Life, Oral Roberts Evangelisitic Association,
   P.O. Box 2187, Tulsa, Oklahoma, 74105.   Formerly
   Healing Waters, changed Sept., 1953; America's Healing
   Magazine, changed Jan., 1956; Healing, changed 1956.
   Monthly. $1.00.
2. Christ for the Nations, Voice of Healing Pub. Co., P.O.
   Box 8658, Dallas, Texas, 75216, monthly   Formerly
   Voice of Healing through April, 1967.
3. The Christian Challenge, Coe Foundations, Inc.   Box
   8538, Dallas, Texas, 75216, monthly.   Formerly
   Herald of Healing and International Healing to June,
   1962.
4. Deeper Life, Morris Cerulla World Evangelism, Inc.,
   4455 Lamont, Box 9525, San Diego, Cal., 92109, monthly.
   $2.00.
5. Faith Digest, T. L. Osborn Evangelistic Assn., 1400
   E. Skelly Dr., Tulsa, Oklahoma, 74102, monthly.
6. Full Gospel News, Full Gospel Evangelisitic Assn.   Box
   431, Webb City, Mo., 64870, monthly.
7. The Healing Messenger, Bible Revival Evangelistic
   Assn.   David Nunn, evangelist.   6626 S. R. L. Thornton
   Fwy.   Dallas, Texas, 75208, monthly.
8. Latter Rain Evangel, Bethesda Missionary Temple, 7570
   E. Nevada Ave., Detroit, Mich.   48234.
9. The March of Faith, Wings of Healing, Inc., Thomas
   Wyatt, 847 S. Grand Ave., Los Angeles, Cal., 90017,
   monthly. $1.00.
10. Miracle Magazine, A. A. Allen Revivals, Inc., Miracle
    Valley, Ariz., monthly.
11. Miracles and Missions Digest, Voice of Miracle and
    Missions, Inc.   M. A. Daud, Box 5646, Dallas, Texas,
    75222, monthly.
12. Revival of America, Leroy Jenkins Evangelisitic Assn.
    Inc., Box F, Delaware, Ohio, 43015, monthly. $1.00.
13. Voice of Deliverance, International Deliverance
    Churches, Jester and Davis St., Dallas, Texas, 75211,
    monthly.
14. A Voice of Faith, Faith Temple Church, Inc., Amman
    Grubb, Box 3220, Memphis, Tenn., 38101, monthly.
15. Word of Faith, Hagin Evangelisitic Assn., Box 50126,
    Tulsa, Oklahoma, 74150, monthly.

IV   Charismatic Periodicals

*1. Charisma Digest, Full Gospel Business Men's Fellowship,
    Int.   836 S. Figueroa St., Los Angeles, Cal., 90017.
    Semi-annual. $1.00.   Discontinued, Jan. 22, 1970.
 2. Cross and the Switchblade, Teen Challenge Publications,
    Box 161, New York, N. Y., 11238.   Bi-monthly.
 3. Heartbeat, Charismatic Educational Centers, Inc., 1730
    S. W. 22nd Ave., Fort Lauderdale, Fla., 33312.   Monthly.

48

4. Logos Journal, Logos International, 185 N. Ave., Plainfield, N. J., 07060. Bi-monthly. $3.00.
5. New Covenant, Charismatic Revival Service P.O. Box 102,
   Main Street Station, Ann Arbor, Mich., 48107. Monthly.
   $5.00.
6. New Nation News, Children of God, Texas Soul Clinic,
   Rt. 1, Mingus, Texas, 76463.
7. New Wine, Holy Spirit Teaching Missions, 1730 S. W.
   22nd Ave., Fort Lauderdale, Fla., 33312. Monthly.
8. Trinity, Blessed Trinity Society, Box 2422, Van Nuys,
   Cal. Quarterly. $5.00. Publication ceased Feb., 1966.
9. Voice, Full Gospel Business Men's Fellowship International, 836 S. Figueron St. Los Angeles, Cal. 90017.
   Monthly. $1.00.

V Missions

1. Full Gospel Native Missionary, Full Gospel Native
   Missionary Assn., Box 1240 Joplin, Mo., 64801. Monthly.
2. Global Witness, United Pentecostal Church, 8855 Dunn
   Road, Hazelwood, Mo., 63042. Monthly.
3. Good News Crusades Assemblies of God, 1445 Boonville
   Ave., Springfield, Mo., 65802. Bi-monthly. Formerly
   Global Conquest through August, 1967
4. The Missionary Voice, Pentecostal Church of God of
   America, Inc., 316 Joplin St., Box 816, Joplin, Mo.
   Monthly.
5. Voice of Revival, Missionary Evangelism, Inc., 1601
   Linda Drive, Decatur, Ga., 30032. Monthly.
6. World Evangelism, American Evangelistic Assn. Box
   4326, Dallas, Texas, 75224. Monthly.
7. World Harvest, World Temples, Inc., Lester Sumrall,
   Box 12, South Bend, Ind., 46624. Monthly.
8. World Vision, Open Bible Standard Churches, 851 19th
   St., Des Moines, Iowa. Quarterly.
9. World o Rama, Pentecostal Holiness Church, Franklin
   Springs, Ga. 30639. Quarterly.

VI Scholarly Journals and Interdenominational Newsletters

1. Academic Forum, Pathway Press, Church of God. 1080
   Montgomery Ave., Cleveland, Tenn., 37311. Quarterly.
2. Paraclete, Gospel Publishing House, Assemblies of God,
   1445 Boonville Ave., Springfield, Mo., 65802. Quarterly. $2.50.

APPENDIX C   (continued)

VII   International and Interdenominational Publications

*1. Pentecost, World Conference of Pentecostal Churches,
    36-37 Clapham Crescent, London, S. W. 4, England.
    Quarterly.   Ceased publication 1966.
 2. P. F. N. A. News, Pentecostal Fellowship of North
    America, 1445 Boonville Ave. Springfield, Mo.,
    65802. Quarterly.
 3. Society for Pentecostal Studies Newsletter, Emmanuel
    College, Box 122, Franklin Springs, Ga., 30639.
    Quarterly. $3.00.
 4. World Pentecost, World Conference of Pentecostal
    Churches. The City Temple, Cowbridge Road, Cardiff,
    Wales, Great Britain. Quarterly. $3.00.

Co-operative Pentecostal Bodies

1. World Pentecostal Fellowship

The WPF was organized in Zurich, Switzerland, in 1947 under
the influence of European Pentecostal Leaders. All Pentecostal groups in the world are eligible to send representa-
tives. The purpose of the meetings is for spiritual fellowship and growth. No form of binding legislation is
attempted. The official journal, Pentecost, ceased publication in 1966 at the death of the editor, Donald Gee.
A new publication, World Pentecost, was authorized at the
ninth World Pentecostal Fellowship, held in Dallas, Texas,
in 1970. Percy Brewster of Wales was selected to be its
editor. The WPF meets triennially.

2. Pentecostal Fellowship of North America

The PFNA organized in October, 1948, at the urging of the
World Pentecostal Fellowship. The statement of faith is
greatly influenced by the National Association of Evangelicals, an organization in which many of the Pentecostal
bodies hold membership. The statement of faith makes it
impossible for the "Oneness" groups to be included. At
present seventeen denominations participate. The PFNA
meets annually.

3. Society for Pentecostal Studies

SPS conducted its first annual meeting in November, 1971,
at Des Moines, Iowa. The purpose of the Society is to
stimulate and promote Pentecostal Scholarship by providing
a forum for discussion of all academic disciplines in
light of Pentecostal theology. The Pentecostal Fellowship
of North America's statement of faith has been adopted by
the Society, to which full members must subscribe. An
occasional Newsletter is published. The society meets
annually.

4. Full Gospel Business Men's Fellowship International

The organization was started in 1951 under the leadership of
Demos Shakarian, a prominent west coast dairy executive.
The purpose of the organization was to stimulate fellowship
among Pentecostal laymen. FGBMFI has proved to be a major
promotional agency of the Charismatic movement. The statement of faith is similar to that of the Pentecostal Fellowship of North America. The organization publishes a
monthly periodical, Voice. More than 425 local chapters
are presently functioning.

APPENDIX D (continued)

5. Teen Challenge

Though Teen Challenge is not a co-operative effort, it is
listed here as the best example to date of Pentecostals'
involvement in today's social problems. Organized in
1958 by David Wilkerson, a minister for the Assemblies
of God, Teen Challenge is geared to meet head-on the drug
problem of America. There are now twenty-seven Teen
Challenge Centers in major U. S. cities, two in Canada,
and four over seas, in addition to rehabilitation farms
and Bible training centers.[26]

---

26. Christianity Today, 16:43, June 23, 1972.

APPENDIX E

Pentecostal Collections[27]

1. The Oral Roberts University Pentecostal Collection is
the most complete. As of January 1, 1972, the collection
contained over 7,000 books, 500 periodicals, five legal
file sets of pamphlet materials, several hundred tapes and
many unpublished theses. Available for purchase are about
forty pages of subject bibliographies, in addition to
the aforementioned bibliography of periodicals.

2. The Archives of the Pentecostal Holiness Church, located
in Franklin Springs, Ga. has an excellent collection of
materials relating to the Holiness-Pentecostal groups
in the south-east.

3. The Archives of the Church of God at denominational
headquarters, Cleveland, Tenn., conatin the best source of
documents for the group of denominations known as the
Church of God.

4. The Pentecostal File of the Assemblies of God, housed
at the headquarters in Springfield, Mo., together with the
collections of Central Bible College and Evangel College
located in the same city, provide excellent materials on
the Keswick groups of Pentecostals.

5. Dr. Walter J. Hollenweger, Department of Theology,
University of Birmingham 815, 277, Bimingham 815, 277
England, has the largest private collection on Pente-
costalism in the world.

6. David J. DuPlessis, 3742 Linwood Ave., Oakland, Cal.,
94602, maintains the best collection of documents relating
to the World Pentecostal Fellowship.

7. Hubert Mitchell of Des Moines, Iowa has the best
source of Pentecostal Fellowship of North America documents.

---

27. For similar listing of collections relating to Pente-
    costalism, consult Vinson Synan, The Holiness-
Pentecostal Movement, p. 225.

INDEX

www.ingramcontent.com/pod-product-compliance
Lightning Source LLC
Chambersburg PA
CBHW020522030426
42337CB00011B/512